W9-CFL-381

THE HISTORY CHANNEL PRESENTS

MODERN MARVELS

INVENTIONS THAT ROCKED THE WORLD

Read all the books in

INVENTIONS THAT ROCKED THE WORLD

By Jane B. Mason and Sarah Hines Stephens

SCHOLASTIC INC.

New York   Toronto   London   Auckland   Sydney

Mexico City   New Delhi   Hong Kong   Buenos Aires

CONTENTS

INVENTIONS ROCK!

You probably ride in a car, a bus, or a train every day. Maybe you use a computer to do your homework and surf the Internet. And you probably talk to your friends on the phone — a lot! But can you imagine life *without* cars, computers, the Internet, or telephones? These inventions play such big roles in our everyday lives that it is practically impossible to think of a world without them. But just over a hundred years ago, *none* of these inventions existed. Back then, most people couldn't imagine what life would be like *with* these innovations! Luckily, a few extraordinary people could.

We've all heard the names Thomas Edison and Benjamin Franklin. These men were two of the brilliant inventors who helped make modern civilization what it is today. Here, you will learn about many other inventors. A simple carpenter invented the first clock that could navigate at sea. And a teacher at a school for the deaf invented the telephone. Inventors come from all walks of life. But what they have in common is a dream — and the willpower to bring that dream to life.

Read on and find out how inventors — from the ancient world to the twenty-first century — took their ingenious ideas, added some hard work and de-termination, and came up with in-ventions that have rocked our world.

Inventing has never been easy. It takes a lot of effort and patience. There are often many obstacles to overcome — along with some strange surprises. But if the inventions and their creators in this book inspire you, perhaps you have it in *you* to become an inventor as well! Grab on to your dream and do not be deterred! A great invention could be right within your grasp. . . .

GETTING THINGS ROLLING:

The Wheel, the Steam Engine, and the Automobile

Try to imagine how people got where they wanted to go before the wheel was invented. They probably walked a lot, which took up a good deal of time! Today, we depend on wheels to get almost everywhere. Without the wheels on cars and buses, how would you get to school? Or visit your friends and faraway relatives? These are all activities we take for granted. How we got wheels, steam engines, and automobiles isn't something we think much about today. But their invention set our lives in motion.

PAVING THE WAY

The wheel, one of history's oldest inventions, paved the way for some of the modern world's greatest innovations, such as the engine and even the airplane!

Nobody knows the exact origin of the wheel, but one of its earliest uses was certainly for transportation. Before farmers had carts, they had to drag their harvests on

Imagine That!

The wheel, together with an axle, was being used for transportation in Mesopotamia as early as 3000 B.C.!

sleds or carry them on their backs! The invention of simple rotary motion — the motion created by using an axle (a pin or shaft that a wheel rotates around) inside a wheel — changed everything.

In a sense, wheels led to the creation of cities. Once farmers could transport crops easily, they could take more food to the people in town. And the more food you could take to a town, the bigger the town could become.

Well-rounded

Transporting food wasn't the only way wheels contributed to the creation of cities. Wheels were extremely versatile. Besides providing basic rotary motion, wheels proved to be helpful with other everyday tasks. Cart wheels were converted into cranks, flywheels, and pulleys, and were used to lift heavy rocks and stones for building. With the help of these wheels, cities grew faster and more efficiently.

Waterwheels were created, too. They were an early source for generating power. And rotating gears — wheels with toothed edges that intermesh so that one wheel drives the other — were essential devices in an endless variety of tools and machinery.

The wheel changed civilization. It had a lasting effect on the way people lived. It also laid the track for another groundbreaking invention: the steam engine.

POUR ON THE STEAM

Legend has it that Scottish instrument maker and engineer James Watt discovered the power of steam in the eighteenth century while he was making tea. Watt observed how the lid on a kettle of boiling water was lifted by steam. But humankind had been aware of steam's power for centuries, long before Watt sat down to that famous cup of tea!

Ancient writings from as early as A.D. 100 described a rotating steam turbine wheel. It was created by a man named Hero of Alexandria and called the "sphere of Aeolus" (Aeolus is the Greek god of the winds). But Hero didn't realize the full potential of his creation. He thought his spinning wheel was nothing more than a "simple toy to keep a drowsy emperor awake." Nearly two thousand years passed before the first practical steam engine was invented.

Around 1712, Thomas Newcomen, an English engineer and inventor, built the first atmospheric steam engine. It consisted of a series of steam-driven piston rods linked by chains that rose and fell while carrying water. The machine was first conceived to pump water out of deep mines. But soon the steam engine was being used for all sorts of things.

Going the Distance

For fifty years, Newcomen's steam engine set the standard. It effectively moved things up and down. But because it didn't run evenly, it was less useful in creating rotary motion, or turning a wheel. So the engineer James Watt set out to improve Newcomen's creation.

Watt bettered the engine by applying steam to both sides of a piston (a solid peg) inside a cylinder (a larger tube), which forced the piston to move back and forth. Using properly designed valves, he created a rocking motion that, with a crank, could be used to rotate a wheel.

The improved steam engine, combined with the wheel, changed the way people traveled over the seas. Steamships were the greatest development in long-distance water travel since the invention of the sail thousands of years before.

The French were the earliest pioneers of

Imagine That!

U.S. roads in the nineteenth century were in poor condition, and horse-drawn carriages moved rather slowly. So *rivers* acted as highways! The advent of steamboats allowed Americans to travel and to ship goods faster than ever before.

steamships. But it was an American, Robert Fulton, who caught the attention of the world with his steamship. In 1807, he powered a commercial steamship line between New York City and Albany, New York.

ALL ABOARD

The success of steam travel on waterways inspired inventors to explore steam engines as a source of power for *land* trans-port as well. This is how the railroad was born.

The very first railroads weren't steam-powered. They were powered by animals that hauled several linked cars on rails. But locomotives with steam engines were stronger and, unlike animals, they didn't require food and rest (just fuel). Steam engines were able to haul heavier loads over greater distances.

By the mid-1800s, the transcontinental railroad connected people across America. Railroads everywhere provided people with mobility, making it easier to travel long distances.

Railways quickly became the world's dominant mode of freight, shipping, and transportation. All around the world, the steam engine allowed cities to grow and develop by delivering people, food, and supplies to waiting doorsteps.

START YOUR ENGINES

By the late 1800s, steam trains and steamships ruled transportation. Still, inventors kept looking for newer, faster, and better ways to move people and things from here to there. And the result was yet another revolutionary invention — the automobile.

Nicolas-Joseph Cugnot, a French inventor, usually gets the credit for inventing the very first car in 1769. With money given to him by the French government, Cugnot built a steam-propelled three-wheeled "artillery wagon." With a top speed of two miles per hour, the wagon wasn't exactly fast. It wasn't very easy to maneuver, either. During a demonstration, the wagon spun out of control and crashed into a wall!

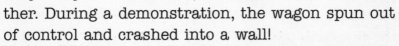

Though Cugnot did invent the first automobile, automaker Karl Benz is known as the "Father of the Automobile." The German inventor is credited with creating the first gasoline-powered road vehicle. In the 1880s, he patented his invention. He then went on to manufacture cars for sale, as did another famous German automaker of the time, Gottlieb Daimler.

TEST YOUR

?

Inventiveness!

Early automobile inventors gave up using steam engines because they were too big. True or false?

Answer: False. They stopped using steam engines because they were too slow, too hot, and too uncomfortable for the passengers seated near the boiler. Youch!

Even when automobiles switched from steam- to gas-powered (also known as internal combustion) engines, steam had not stopped "heating up" the wheel. It was an early steam engine that inspired one of history's most famous automotive pioneers, Henry Ford. Ford was just a boy when he saw his first self-powered vehicle. It had a profound effect on him. And later, *he* would have a profound effect on the entire automobile industry.

Imagine That!

If you've come up with a cool and useful invention, it is a good idea to *patent* it. A patent is a document that grants rights to produce and sell a specific item. If an inventor doesn't file a patent at the patent office, anyone can make and sell his or her invention.

Get in Line

Henry Ford's greatest achievement was making cars that people could afford. In the early 1900s there were a number of companies manufacturing automobiles, but it was Ford who first developed a car that was cheap enough to sell to the general public. It was called the Model T.

The Model T was affordable because it was built on an assembly line. Ford did not invent the assembly line — he borrowed it from another industry. In fact, the source of his inspiration was pretty gruesome: the meatpacking industry! Meatpackers worked on what was often called the "disassembly line" — conveyor belts that moved animal carcasses down a line. Along the way, the carcass was taken apart by cutters at different stations.

Imagine That!

The Model T was also known as the "Tin Lizzy."

Putting together a car was a lot more complicated than cutting up meat. To use the assembly line method, Ford needed interchangeable parts. He also had to carefully choreograph the movements of all the pieces before they came together. Transmissions and engines and axles were assembled on their own lines before they were brought to the big line. In the end, everything came together and a brandnew Model T rolled out of the factory!

Hit the Road

Before halting production in 1927, Ford made seventeen million Model T's! During that time other car manufacturers used Ford's innovations and soon a whole array of affordable automobiles became available, including other Ford models.

Cars soon became enormously popular — and obviously, they still are! Today there are nearly 300 million cars in the United States alone. Although the Ford company is still a well-known producer of cars, there are now countless car manufacturers across the globe

Inventiveness!

In the 1920s, when the assembly line was in full force, the price of a Model T dropped down to $2,600. True or false?

Answer: False. It dropped from $850 (that was a huge amount of money at the time) to just $260.

who continue to innovate and surprise us with exciting and interesting models. Today's cars can be sleek and shiny, or big and impressive, but they all serve the same purpose — to get us from place to place safely and quickly!

The car may be the most influential invention of the twentieth century. It changed the landscape by getting people to put down paved roads and create highway systems. It changed our lives by allowing us to travel wherever and whenever we want in privacy.

The car, the railroad, the steamship, and the steam engine are all inventions with lasting impact. They revolutionized transportation and made an industrial revolution possible. And they share a simple origin: It was the humble wheel that got them all rolling!

Imagine That!

The period of time between 1750 and 1850 is often referred to as the Industrial Revolution. Across the world, inventions and new technology made factories and large-scale production possible. People moved in large numbers from farms and small towns to urban centers.

The Industrial Revolution provided nations with a stronger economic base and improved living standards for many. But it also introduced new problems like pollution and overcrowding.

A FLIP OF THE SWITCH:
Electricity, the Telegraph, and the Telephone

When you walk into a dark room, what's the first thing you do? Chances are you flip a switch that turns on a bright light overhead. It's thanks to the amazing invention of electricity that you are able to do this. But before we were able to control electricity, people relied on candles for light — or got used to living in the dark!

Electricity did much more than bring light into our lives. Like the wheel, it led to other groundbreaking innovations — in particular, various means of communication that still connect us today.

WE'VE GOT THE POWER

Researchers today have learned that scientists in ancient Greece actually knew how to create electricity. They would rub amber (which is "electron" in ancient Greek) until it attracted lightweight objects, like feathers. They did this just for amusement. Even though ancient Greeks could create and observe electricity, they could not harness — or control — it. Not until a few hundred years ago did humans discover a way to contain electricity's incredible power.

You've probably heard the famous story about Benjamin Franklin and his kite. Franklin was a celebrated thinker, politician, and inventor. In 1752, he flew a kite in an electrical storm as an experiment. When Franklin noticed the threads of his kite string standing on end, he touched the metal key he had tied to the string. Though Franklin got quite a *shock*, he was not really surprised. He had proven his theory — that electricity was stored in the clouds in the form of lightning.

Using his new knowledge, Franklin went on to invent the lightning rod. A metal rod that works as a conductor, it directs lightning down it and into the ground. When placed on a rooftop, the lightning rod prevented a home from catching on fire if it was struck by lightning.

What Franklin showed the world with his kite — and the lightning rod — was that electricity could be directed and controlled. Other scientists hoped to not only direct but also *store* the awesome force for later use. So they set out to invent what would eventually become the battery.

Imagine That!

When lightning rods began to appear on homes across the country, many church officials opposed the invention. They believed that lightning expressed the wrath of God and shouldn't be tampered with!

High Voltage

The first battery, as we know it, did not appear until the 1800s. This early energy-storage device was created by Italian inventor Alessandro Volta, and it looked like a big pile of plates.

The voltaic pile, as it is sometimes called, consisted of alternating plates made of copper and zinc with an acid between them (Volta used pads soaked in salt water). The chemical reaction caused by the acid created a charge of electrical potential that flowed through the alternating plates. The strength of this potential was measured in volts (named after Volta, of course!).

Volta's invention was groundbreaking. It allowed people to store powerful electricity so it could be used as a source of energy. Since then, improvements have been made to the battery, and many different types of batteries have been created. One of them, known as the wet cell, was basically a jar of acid with electrodes (metal conductors) stuck inside it. The acid caused a chemical reaction that pro-

TEST YOUR

Inventiveness!

The very first battery was invented in the sixteenth century. True or false?

Answer: False. Scientists believe that the first crude electrical battery may have been invented in the first century A.D.

duced electrons (electric particles), which flowed through the metal electrodes.

Batteries provide power to an endless range of devices. Today we use batteries to operate almost everything! We put dry cell (alkaline) batteries in watches, flashlights, and remote-control toys so that they can "run" for hours and hours. We recharge wet cell batteries in our mobile phones and portable computers. And we start our cars using heavy-duty lead batteries.

Just like people today, inventors years ago

found the battery to be an indispensable device. It quickly became a key component in all sorts of experiments. You might even call the battery *illuminating*!

LIGHTEN UP!

With the invention of the battery, scientists learned to harness small amounts of electrical energy. In their quest for stronger, more powerful currents of electricity, inventors were continually finding new ways to generate electrical power. These findings led to other inventions. One of these inventions literally brought the world out of the "dark ages," turning night into day. It was the simple but life-changing lightbulb.

The search for usable light dates back to the 1830s. Then, people were looking for an alternative to the smoky and dangerous gas and oil lamps that were being used at that time.

The principle was simple. Everyone could see that heated objects — like logs on a fire — glow and emit light. The problem was finding how one could control that light.

By the 1870s, scientists could create electrical arcs, like lightning, between two carbon poles. These extremely bright lights were used in streetlamps. But since there was no way to control the luminosity, or brightness, they were not well-suited for homes.

Inventors around the world were working to create a viable lightbulb. And a few did. But it was the already-famous inventor of the phonograph — Thomas Alva Edison — who was given credit for the first successful bulb.

The Brilliant Mr. Edison

Edison was always very sure of himself. He boasted that his lightbulb would be ready in only a few months. It took him over a year, but he did in fact produce a light-bulb.

Thin carbon was the key, Edison discovered, to getting a bulb that glowed brightly, but not too brightly. He made a very thin carbon string between the two poles inside an airtight bulb. When he ran an electrical

Imagine That!

Thomas Edison is usually credited with inventing the lightbulb in 1879. But a British inventor, Joseph Wilson Swan, had unveiled a filament lamp not unlike Edison's nearly a year earlier!

current through the bulb, it produced adequate light for a room in a house.

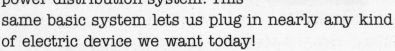

Edison's invention of the lightbulb in 1879 profoundly changed society, literally illuminating our world. A visionary inventor, Edison saw even beyond the lightbulb. Within a year he had laid the groundwork for a complete electrical light and power distribution system. This same basic system lets us plug in nearly any kind of electric device we want today!

The lightbulb was a small invention with a huge impact. Light inside factories allowed for overnight work and increased production. Light made transportation at night possible. It revolutionized entertainment and advertising. There was hardly an aspect of daily life that the lightbulb did not affect.

SNAIL MAIL

Less than 150 years ago, communication was mostly limited to messages delivered in person.

There were no telegraphs, no phones, no e-mail, and certainly no instant messaging!

Before the telegraph and the telephone, people had to think of creative ways to communicate over distance. They set up flag towers, sent smoke signals, and used carrier pigeons. But these methods were too slow and not very dependable.

As scientific knowledge grew and people realized that electricity could be transferred from one place to another, they began to experiment with the possibility that the same principle could be applied to communication.

The result was an invention that would bring the world closer together. It

Imagine That!

Delays in communication could sometimes have disastrous results. The greatest battle of the War of 1812 was fought *after* peace had already been reached between Great Britain and America. Word of the peace agreement did not reach the soldiers in time to stop the conflict!

was the first instant communication device — the telegraph.

Dots and Dashes

Based on the battery and the electromagnet (both invented in the early nineteenth century), in the 1840s the telegraph was simply a wire strung over a set distance. The telegraph wire was connected to an electromagnet on one end and an on/off switch on the other. Turning the switch on sent a charge down the wire. The charge moved a pencil, making a series of marks at the receiving end. A dash-and-dot code represented numbers and letters. The telegraph allowed people to send any message they wanted over any distance. But it had one major drawback: It depended on a physical wire link. You could only send messages between spots that had a wire running between them.

When word of the

Imagine That!

Samuel Morse, the inventor of the Morse code of dots and dashes, was the first person to successfully send a telegraph message in 1844. The demonstration line was set up between Washington, D.C., and Baltimore, Maryland, and the message was both simple and powerful: "What hath God wrought?"

telegraph's quick communication capability got out, people quickly began laying down wires. The growth of the telegraph was dramatic. By 1855, thirty thousand miles of telegraph wire had been strung. There were stations in almost every major American city. Just twenty years after Samuel Morse sent the first telegraph message, undersea Atlantic cables were laid down to transmit messages between continents! The telegraph was being used to send not just personal messages but also news and even warnings.

TEST YOUR

Inventiveness!

The telegraph was sometimes used for catching criminals. True or false?

Answer: True. In Great Britain, a prisoner tried to escape by train, but railroad officials telegraphed ahead to the next station and gave them the criminal's exact description and seat location! He was easily apprehended.

CAN YOU HEAR ME NOW?

The telegraph opened inventors' eyes to new possibilities. It also created some frustrations that would lead the way to the next inventive step.

To send telegraphic messages required two operators *and* a trip to the telegraph office. Plus, only one message could be sent and decoded at a time.

It lacked the easy back and forth of a human conversation.

The telephone was the next logical step. In fact, the phone's inventor, Alexander Graham Bell, called his device a "speaking telegraph." And that is exactly what the first telephone was — a telegraph line with a microphone and speaker on each end.

Bell discovered that electrical currents could duplicate sound waves. By vibrating in a series of frequencies, electrical currents could send not just tones but multiple sounds — or even one complex sound wave, the human voice.

Mr. Watson, Come Here!

Bell and his assistant, Thomas Watson, worked hard to perfect their theories of re-creating sound waves through wire. And in March 1876, they finally did.

The story of the first phone call has grown into a legend. Bell was working alone in a room on a transmitter. Watson was in another room with the receiver. The transmitter appeared to be functioning. "Mr. Watson, come here! I want to see you!"

Bell said, and his words traveled through the phone line.

This exciting moment in history seemed a little too boring to Watson, who liked to invent (or at least embellish) stories as much as he liked to invent gadgets. In a speech years later, Watson added more drama to the call. He reported that Bell had spilled battery acid on his leg and cried out for his assistant to aid him. Voilà! The first emergency phone call had been placed. And Watson's more exciting story is the one most often repeated.

Imagine That!

Alexander Graham Bell's mother was almost completely deaf, and her lack of hearing had a huge influence on him. Bell worked as a teacher for the deaf. And though he tried for years to invent a hearing aid, he never did. However, his research on sound waves helped him to invent the telephone.

Somebody Get the Phone!

As amazing as telephones and instant person-to-person communication were, the phone did not catch on right away. Though the phone turned out to be one of the most lucrative patents ever, the leading communications giant of the time — Western Union — refused Bell's offer to sell it to them.

Little by little, the public gravitated toward the phone. And even Western Union began to rethink their decision. In 1877, they offered to buy the telephone from Bell Telephone Company. Bell refused. By then he knew he had a good thing.

TEST YOUR

Inventiveness!

Bell once used a real human ear removed from a cadaver to research and develop the telephone. True or false?

Answer: True! He got it from a physician friend.

WHAT POWER!

Bulbs, batteries, and telephones are simple to use and an ordinary part of our lives. But the next time you talk on your cell phone or turn on a flashlight at night, just think: At the tip of your fingers there is the power that scientists throughout the ages struggled to harness — and finally did!

The early locomotive engine (above) revolutionized travel. It also inspired the invention of the modern automobile, such as this Lamborghini Countach (below). Both the steam-engine train and the car owe their existence to the same amazing, ancient invention: the wheel!

F920 OYR

These are images of just a few of history's greatest inventors. Alexander Graham Bell was the innovative mind behind the "speaking telegraph," which would go on to become the present-day telephone. Thomas Alva Edison's brilliant contributions include the carbon filament incandescent lightbulb and motion pictures—no wonder he was known as a "wizard"! Benjamin Franklin was more than just an inventor—he was also a politician and author. Henry Ford was a pioneer who used the assembly-line method to make cars that were more affordable.

Alexander Graham Bell (1847–1922)

Thomas Alva Edison (1847–1931)

Benjamin Franklin (1706–1790)

Since all these inventors were creative thinkers and hard workers, they embody Edison's famous saying: "Genius is one percent inspiration and ninety-nine percent perspiration."

Henry Ford (1863–1947)

 THE HISTORY CHANNEL

We've come a long way! The early telephone (above), a large and often heavy communication device, evolved into the contemporary sleek and light cellular phone (below). Who knows how the phone—or other means of communication—will continue to change and improve in the future?

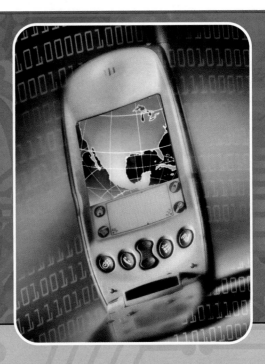

It may be hard to believe, but the man fiddling with the mass of wires (above) is working with the first general-purpose computer, at the U.S. Army's Aberdeen Proving Ground in Maryland. Built in the 1940s, this computer weighed thirty tons and was eight feet high and one hundred feet long. The computers we use today, of course, have undergone some incredible changes. The lightweight, portable laptop (below) is the barely recognizable "descendant" of the early computer!

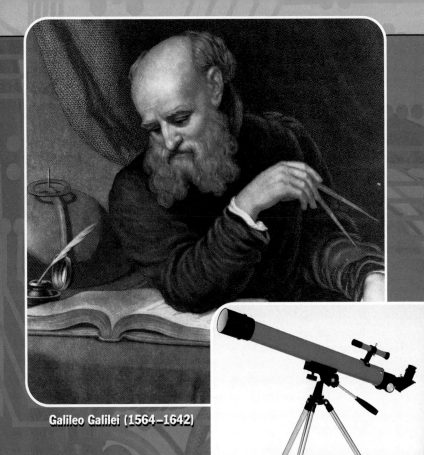

Galileo Galilei (1564–1642)

THE HISTORY CHANNEL. The Italian physicist Galileo Galilei was the first to use the newly invented telescope to study the heavens. The modern-day telescope (such as the one shown at right) continues to teach astronomers and scientists about the stars and planets. Just peer through the lens and you, too, could learn some secrets about our solar system....

(top) Corbis; (bottom) David Waitz/SODA

This is the mechanism of an antique clock, a behind-the-scenes look at how a clock really works. You can see the rotating gears with teeth that make up the essential part of any functioning mechanical clock. The mechanical clock was invented in the thirteenth century, and was the first man-made device that was able to accurately tell time.

The Chinese magic spoon was an ancient "gadget" used only for amusement. But because the spoon, which was made from magnetite, could point in specific directions, it evolved into a useful invention: the compass, an example of which is shown here. The compass was invented to help sailors navigate at sea. Today it is still used by travelers and explorers—which just goes to show, a gadget can sometimes morph into a tool that changes our lives!

WATCH OUT:
Radio, Movies, TV, and Computers

Think of a typical afternoon. You come home after school, switch on the radio, and start your homework. When you need to look something up, you turn on the computer and surf the Web. All finished? It's time to relax in front of the TV, or maybe meet your friends at the movie theater. Radios, televisions, computers, and movie screens are *everywhere*, providing us with information and entertainment anytime we want. But it wasn't always this way. . . .

RADIO ACTIVE!

When the concept of radio was introduced early in the twentieth century, it created a kind of revolution. The very idea of sending messages through the air without wires was amazing. The radio was the first device to bring instant information and entertainment into the home, making it one of history's most enjoyable inventions.

Invisible Waves

The key element of radio is, of course, the radio wave. Radio waves are invisible electromagnetic waves of energy. In the 1860s, a physicist named James Clerk Maxwell described these waves, but he was not able to create them. About twenty years later another scientist, Heinrich Hertz, actually produced radio waves. After that, it *still* took several scientists twenty or so *more* years to come up with a way to send and receive these waves through the air.

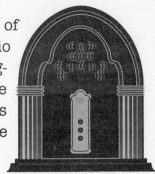

A Bright Idea

Can you guess which earlier inventions provided the inspiration for the radio? Its more obvious "ancestors" are the telegraph and telephone — devices used for communication over distance. But its less obvious relative is the lightbulb.

An Italian inventor named Guglielmo Marconi converted a lightbulb into a vacuum tube — one of the key workings of a radio. The vacuum tube proved to be efficient in detecting and producing radio waves. It worked as both a transmitter and a receiver, sending messages through the air from one place and picking them up in another.

After Marconi proved that radio waves could travel through air, he added a simple sound signal, like the Morse code. And in 1898, he sent a radio transmission nearly twenty miles across the English Channel. It was the first wireless transmission.

Going Wireless

The new wireless telegraph brought about big changes. Before radio transmissions, long-distance communication had to be sent through wires that were laid by hand. But with the advent of radios, ships could send distress signals from the middle of the ocean!

By the 1920s, voice transmissions had replaced coded signals. People everywhere could hear news instantly on radios. A new era of mass communication was born. By the 1940s, radio had captured the imagination of the world. The device could be found in most homes and was used for both information and entertainment. But radios weren't like the current stereo systems we are used to. Radios in the forties were much bigger — around four feet high — and often took center stage in the living room.

A PICTURE IS WORTH A THOUSAND INVENTORS

Inventors rarely stop inventing after they hit on something good. They just keep thinking of ways to make it better! Seeing that sound could travel over great distances, scientists began to wonder if they could send *visual* images as well. The result of their wonderings — and a lot of work — was the television.

The modern TV was not the product of a single inventor. Numerous inventors throughout history and around the world had a hand in its creation.

It was Leonardo da Vinci, the great Italian artist and inventor, who discovered, in the 1500s, that the human eye continues to see an image for a fraction of a second after it disappears. Based on that concept, modern televisions show thirty still pictures every second, but our eyes view a constant moving image!

Without Sir Isaac Newton's work we might not have color TV. In 1666, he discovered the color spectrum and proved that a rainbow of colors is formed when white light is shone through a glass prism.

Vladimir Zworykin and Philo Farnsworth are the scientists most often credited with the invention of electronic TV. Working independently in the United States, they invented a way to detect an image electrically, store it within a vacuum tube, and send it electrically to a receiver. The receiver then converted the stored image to electrons. And the image was reproduced when the electrons hit a phosphorus screen — a TV!

Imagine That!

Though television was invented in the 1920s, it took many years to catch on. In 1936, only two thousand television sets were used around the world. By 1955, more than thirty million homes had TVs!

Changing History, Changing Channels

Television changed communication completely. It allowed us to watch history in the making. It changed not just the way we view the world but also the way we think about it. It created a way for us to share information and experiences with millions of people all at the same time. Today we have hundreds of channels, each one suited to a different taste or purpose. There are so many kinds of programming that we have channels dedicated exclusively to

news, shopping, fish-
ing, home improve-
ment, and, of course,
history!

MOVIE MAGIC

Like television,
movies can inform
and entertain. But

when you step into a dark-
ened theater you are transported. More than TV,
motion pictures draw you in and hold you spell-
bound. (Think of that funny rub-your-eyes feeling
when you come out of a matinee and are surprised
by daylight!)

Moving Pictures

People's fascina-
tion with moving
and illuminated
pictures can be
traced back as
far as the 1600s.
A device called
the magic lantern
was documented
in a book by a Je-

TEST YOUR

Inventiveness!

On July 20, 1969, more than 600
million viewers around the world
watched the first television
transmission from the moon.
True or false?

Answer: True.

suit priest. It was a kind of old-fashioned slide projector that shone light through painted glass pictures.

In the 1860s, the zoetrope was popular. Invented by William George Horner in 1834, the zoetrope created the illusion of movement. When the viewer looked through slots at spinning sequential images, they appeared to be moving.

Like a combination of the magic lantern and the zoetrope, movies project sequential images. The still photographs appear to move because our eyes synthesize, or fill in, the differences.

Another key element in movies is photography. Louis Jacques Mandé Daguerre perfected the "magical" technology of photography in 1829. But capturing images on light-sensitive glass plates was a slow process. You might need as much as five minutes to take just one picture. By the 1870s, faster picture taking was possible, and it captured the inventor Thomas Edison's imagination.

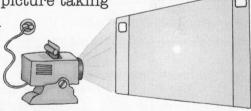

The Wizard of Menlo Park

Not many people would deny that movies are a great invention. But who first thought of showing stories on a big screen? Was it the legendary inventor Thomas Edison? That is something that is still up for debate.

That Edison was an amazing inventor is undeniable. In fact, you've already read about him and his work on the lightbulb. Even while he was alive, Edison had a legendary quality. He was called the "Wizard of Menlo Park" (the location of his laboratories). People believed Edison could do anything, as did Edison himself!

Although Edison is often given credit as the sole inventor of the motion picture, there were many other people involved — including one person who was right in Edison's own lab!

A Little Help

Edison hired William Kennedy Laurie Dickson, a trusted assistant and avid photographer, to head up his motion picture project. Edison named his new project the "kinetoscope," from the Greek words for "motion" and "view."

Because he worked on several projects at once, Edison was rarely in his lab. Dickson worked alone, often for long hours, developing the technology.

Something Borrowed

In the late 1800s, people in other parts of the world had similar ideas about inventing a moving picture. In France, Etienne-Jules Marey developed a camera that could take sequential photos. A revolving cylinder on his camera allowed him to take a series of pictures on a strip of film.

Edison, always looking for a way to improve his own projects, met with Marey. When Edison returned home, he suggested Dickson use perforated strips of film that moved through the camera.

In 1891, Dickson arranged a surprise premiere for Edison's wife and her luncheon guests. The women looked into a wooden box and saw a flickering image of Dickson removing his hat!

After that, Dickson worked feverishly to perfect the mechanism

Imagine That!

Dickson created the first-ever movie studio at Edison's laboratories. It was a dark and often hot room called the Black Maria. It was built on a rotating platform to catch the sun's light.

so it could be introduced to the public. Dickson was the designer, engineer, projectionist, and even the actor in his early films.

Kinetoscopes quickly became all the rage. Kinetoscope parlors popped up all over, and people went to them to watch short movies and even boxing matches through the holes in the wooden boxes. But by 1895 people wanted more. They wanted the "big screen."

Big Screen

Dickson encouraged Edison to work on a projected movie that could be shown to many people at once — the big screen. But Edison didn't want to replace something that was working. He was making money from the kinetoscope.

Frustrated, Dickson began secretly working with Edison's competitors. But when Dickson's activities were discovered, he was forced to leave Edison's lab.

Other inventors continued to look for ways to improve moving pictures. In France, two brothers, Auguste and Louis Jean Lumière, invented a hand-cranked movie camera. And on December 28, 1895, they were the first to publicly project a movie onto a large screen.

In America, just ahead of the Lumières, Charles

Francis Jenkins and Thomas Armat demonstrated their projection system. Edison, seeing that he had missed the boat, quickly put his name on the system and debuted it publicly on April 23, 1896. Edison would forever be remembered as the inventor of motion pictures.

Imagine That!

Old movies are often called silent pictures because they didn't have synchronized sound. But silent films were never really silent. Live offstage sound effects were used, as well as music from a single piano or even a whole orchestra.

Sight and Sound

Edison felt it was very important to make sound a part of movies. In 1912 Edison linked his phonograph with movie equipment, creating the kinetophone. It was introduced in theaters to gasps of astonishment, but soon lost its appeal. It was hard to keep the sound and the picture in sync, and audiences jeered at the mismatched sound and images.

But after many more years of work, the vitaphone sound system was invented. This allowed for sound to merge more gracefully with the images on film.

The year 1927 brought Thomas Edison's eightieth birthday. It also brought the first successful "talking picture," *The Jazz Singer*. From that time on, the motion picture industry prospered, and of course, continues to thrive today.

TINY TRANSISTOR

Radios and television were amazing inventions, but these items depended on big, bulky, expensive, and unreliable vacuum tubes for their power.

Then, in 1948, an invention the size of a finger was quietly introduced. The transistor may have been tiny, but it made a huge impact.

Three men — John Bardeen, Walter Brattain, and William Shockley — were working in the Bell Telephone Laboratories (part of the AT&T phone company) when they invented the transistor. They needed the small electronic machine because they used a lot of information circuitry (electrical storage components) in their phone systems and didn't want the phones to be too bulky.

The transistor worked by strengthening electrical signals. By releasing a surge of electrons through the transistor, a weak electrical signal was transformed into a much stronger copy of itself. It was a simple solution and took up a fraction of the space of vacuum tubes. The transistor scaled everything down in size.

Although nobody paid much attention when the transistor was introduced at a press conference in New York, eventually its creators were awarded the Nobel Prize in physics. And their invention triggered one of the most sweeping technological revolutions in history.

CHIP OFF THE OLD TRANSISTOR

The transistor played a key role in the invention of something that impacts our lives at school, work, and home every day: the computer. Tens of millions of transistors are contained on an integrated circuit or computer chip — the tiny part of a computer that runs the *whole* thing!

Early Computers

The earliest computers were created by a French mathematician named Blaise Pascal. In 1645, he invented a machine that

Imagine That!

The first computers used eighteen thousand vacuum tubes and filled a large room! Today's small computers have tens of millions of microscopic transistors on a single chip.

could compute math problems. Pascal thought his invention was great. He thought mathematicians would line up for his new device. To his surprise, the invention was rejected. People feared the new device would cost them their jobs.

Pascal was so disappointed that he gave up his life's work. But others continued working on computers. In the 1850s, a British mathematician named Charles Babbage invented a mechanical device that closely resembled today's computers.

Keeping Count

The next big advancement came from Herman Hollerith. Hollerith invented a punched card computing system to aid in the census, the population count taken in the United States every ten years.

In 1911, Hollerith's company merged with another to form the Computer Tabulating Recording Company. In 1924, they changed their name to International Business Machines Corporation, better known as IBM. Forty years later IBM introduced the IBM 360. The 360 and its descendants were the first popular personal computers.

In the 1970s, two men named Steve Jobs and Steve Wozniak built and sold their own computers out of a garage in California. These two Steves later formed the company now known as Apple. And by 1977, Apple computers were  starting to threaten IBM's hold on the market. In 1980, Apple controlled half of the personal computer market.

Today, lots of companies compete for personal computer sales. And computers can be found in businesses, schools, libraries, and homes. We use them to work, play, and get information. But one of their most popular uses is for communication.

CAUGHT IN THE NET

The Internet is a global computer communications network that practically makes the telegraph look like a tin-can telephone! Development of this information transfer system started in the 1960s. The United States Department of Defense was looking for a way to allow researchers to share the use of supercomputers. The Advanced Research Project Agency (ARPA) created a network that allowed computers to link up via phone lines and satellites. Once they were linked, the computers could send bits of information back and forth. It was called the ARPANET and was the early predecessor of the Internet.

Although students and researchers started to use the ARPANET for e-mail in the 1970s, the Internet as we know it wasn't born until the 1980s. That's when the combination of inexpensive personal computers and a variety of network servers, which link computers to the Internet, created a boom.

Welcome to the World Wide Web

The 1990s brought the World Wide Web. You can think of the Web as a global collection of interconnected text and multimedia (video, picture, and text) files.

The Web caught on faster than a spider catches flies. By 1997, the number of computers with Web access was approaching ten million!

Today many people are able to telecommute on the Internet. They can do their work over the computer so

they don't have to travel to an office. Some people can even work from their homes! The Internet allows us to easily do research, take classes, get information, and communicate quickly and easily with people all over the world.

SMALL WORLD, AFTER ALL

You might not think your radio, TV, computer, and local movie theater have much in common. But all of these incredible inventions do one thing — they help people communicate. They bring people together. Just as wheels and engines brought about big social changes, radios, televisions, movies, and especially computers have ushered in a new age: the Information Age. Today we have more access to information than ever before. And people are able to stay in touch with greater ease. With the advent of e-mail, you can talk to a friend a continent away, send pictures to him or her instantly, even discuss a movie you have both seen! And the ability to do all that *definitely* makes the world seem like a smaller place.

AWESOME INSTRUMENTS:
The Clock, the Telescope, and the Microscope

People have always been eager to learn about the world around them. But studying our surroundings hasn't always been easy. A long time ago, scientists didn't have the tools to measure things, or to get an up-close look.

Today we are lucky enough to have incredibly accurate instruments at our disposal. A peek at your watch will tell you the exact time, down to the second. And if looking at the stars and planets strikes your fancy, you can peer through a telescope. Meanwhile, tiny things that exist here on Earth — such as germs, bacteria, and cells that are invisible to the human eye — can now be magnified and examined through the lens of a microscope.

Clocks, telescopes, and microscopes have not only helped us to be more accurate about our surroundings — their discovery has revolutionized science and medicine. But how did these awe-inspiring instruments come to be? Read on to find out. . . .

DO YOU HAVE THE TIME?

Nowadays, we use mechanical clocks to monitor the minutes and hours that pass. But long before clocks had been invented, ancient peoples used sand, shadows, water, and even giant structures to keep track of time.

The ancient, mysterious monument Stonehenge can be found in southern England. Its huge stones weigh many tons and form a circle. Nobody knows exactly how Stonehenge came to be. How were the stones cut into pillarlike shapes? How were they transported and set upright? Though we're not sure how Stonehenge was

built, we do know, at least in part, *why*. The stones were arranged so that they would be directly aligned with the sun on important dates, such as the summer solstice (the longest day of the year). The stones form a sort of early calendar.

Ancient Egyptians used huge obelisks — slim, tapered pillars —

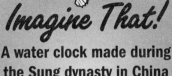

Imagine That!

A water clock made during the Sung dynasty in China had a huge wooden waterwheel that jumped ahead every fifteen minutes when one of its water buckets filled up. It stood thirty feet high!

to mark time. These pillars were hundreds of feet tall! The columns cast shadows onto circular

patterns on the ground. Different patterns represented different times of day.

The Greeks and Romans used smaller sundials to tell time. When a sundial is aligned with the sun in the correct way, the sun's shadow falls on the exact time of day on a dial. The part of the sundial that casts the shadow is called a gnomon (NO-mon).

Moving on to Mechanics

Throughout most of the Middle Ages, the methods used to tell time were not entirely accurate. But during the thirteenth century, a revolutionary new way to measure time was born — the mechanical clock.

A mechanical clock has many behind-the-scenes parts. But the most important are the rotating gears with teeth, the escapement, the regulating device, and the hands that we look at to tell time.

All mechanical clocks feature several gears with teeth. These gears always do the same thing: turn at different but consistent rates, one tooth at a time. These controlled turns move the hands on the clock's face, ticking off the hours and minutes of the day.

The escapement is the important middleman in the "engine" of a mechanical clock. Usually a

Imagine That!

A water clock called a clepsydra (clep-SEHD-reh) was used in ancient Greece to time lawyers' arguments in court. Water dripped through a hole at the bottom, filling a bowl in fifteen minutes. When the bowl was full, your time was up!

falling weight or an unwinding spring, it connects the gears to the regulating device.

A good example of a regulating device is the pendulum on a grandfather clock. It swings back and forth at the same rate, making an audible ticktock. This regulator controls the hands and how fast they move.

LOST AT SEA

In the early 1700s, British, French, and Spanish ships went to sea in droves. They also got lost in droves — because as soon as they lost sight of land, there was no way for the sailors to know where they were.

In order to navigate, sailors needed to know both their latitude (north–south position) and their longitude (east–west

Imagine That!

A man named Seth Atwood traveled all over the world collecting clocks. They took up so much room in his house that he decided to open a museum! Called the Time Museum, it housed roughly 1,500 clocks until it closed in 1999.

position). Figuring out their latitude was easy — they just had to measure the height of the sun or stars above the horizon. But figuring out their longitude was much more difficult.

The clever minds of the time knew it was possible to determine longitude with a clock. If you set a clock to the time in the home port, you would be able to tell how far east or west you'd traveled by observing the time difference between noon (when the sun is directly above you) at your location and noon on the clock. But in order for this to work, you'd need a clock that was accurate, even when it was tossed around by the waves at sea. At this time, there was not a clock in the world that could do this.

In the 1720s, carpenter John Harrison decided to build an accurate sea clock. It was no easy task. It took him four years just to come up with the design. Then it took him another five years to build it!

Called the H-1, the first sea clock was three feet high and three feet wide. It weighed seventy pounds! The clock used seesaw balances connected to metal ribbons. These balances and ribbons could be turned in any direction — even upside down — and still rock the same way. The clock was not affected by gravity!

Everyone in London flocked to see the amazing

H-1. But Harrison was his own worst critic. He knew he could make a *better* sea clock. Over the next nineteen years he built three more clocks: H-2, H-3, and H-4. While doing so, he made a breakthrough discovery. He learned that a small clock with a high-frequency balance was a lot more stable than a bigger clock.

Harrison's round H-4 clock was roughly four inches in diameter, the size of a large pocket watch. But the timepiece was amazingly accurate. After its six-week test voyage to Jamaica, it was running only five seconds slow!

TEST YOUR

Inventiveness!

Determining longitude at sea was such a vexing problem that the British government offered a prize of ten thousand pounds (the equivalent of at least a million dollars today) to the person who could solve it. True or false?

Answer: False. There was indeed such a contest, but the prize money was twenty thousand pounds!

CLOCK-MAKING MANIA

In the early 1800s, clock making changed dramatically. A clock maker named Eli Terry was hired to make four thousand clocks in three years. Nobody thought it was possible.

At the time, clocks were still made one at a time. Each one was individual and unique. Eli Terry changed all of that. He developed a clock-making plant that would produce thousands of clocks out of interchangeable parts.

Terry spent the first two years setting up a factory and an assembly line. He didn't make a single clock until the third year. But he filled the entire clock order. And by mass-producing so many clocks, he brought clocks and watches into the hands of the common people, who until then could not afford them.

Imagine That!

In the 1700s, the French made clocks that were so ornate that the time period has been called the golden age of clock making.

Wrist Rage

In the late 1800s, wearing a timekeeper on the wrist became quite popular — but only for women. No self-respecting man would consider wearing a wristwatch. He would only carry a pocket watch. But World War I (from 1914 to 1918) changed all that.

During battle, it was too complicated to remove a watch from one's pocket to find out what time it was. A soldier needed to keep his hands free for other things. Watchmakers began to advertise the convenience of wrist-watches, and sales took off.

After the war, everyone suddenly wanted a wristwatch. Factories all over the world began to churn them out. And Swiss watchmakers produced the thinnest, most stylish watches. Before long, Switzerland controlled sixty percent of the world's wristwatch market.

These days, watches have all kinds of cool features. They come in every color and shape. They can glow in the dark, tell the date, and have fancy stop-watch features. Some can even measure your heart rate!

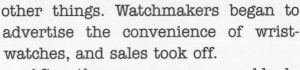

TEST YOUR

Inventiveness!

Early wristwatches for men were actually small pocket watches with loops soldered on to allow for straps. True or false?

Answer: True.

Supercool Quartz

In 1928, two Americans, J. W. Horton and W. A. Morrison, invented yet another kind of timekeeper: the quartz clock. This clock was based on the back-

and-forth movement of a tiny quartz crystal. When an electric current was applied to the quartz, it vibrated at a constant frequency. With no gears or escapements to disturb its regular, repeating motion, the quartz clock is amazingly accurate.

Later, in the 1950s, an even more accurate timekeeper was developed: the atomic clock. This clock used the back-and-forth motions of the particles inside a cesium atom to measure time.

Imagine That!

Since workers in Industrial Revolution England didn't have alarm clocks, they hired "knockers-up." The knockers-up were people who would tap on the worker's window an hour before the factory shift started.

The most recent atomic clock is called the hydrogen master. The incredible hydrogen master has been used in all kinds of fields. Doctors use it in medical equipment. It's used in satellites that track Earth-tide measurements. And astronomers use it to maintain telescope controls.

STAR LIGHT, STAR BRIGHT

Look up at the sky. There's a whole world up there! A world of stars, planets, galaxies, and more. Astronomers have learned a lot about our solar system and the heavenly bodies that shine above us. We've sent rockets into space, taken pictures of other planets, even walked on the moon.

Until four hundred years ago, we knew very little about our solar system. Not because we weren't interested, but because there was no way to look closely at objects millions of miles above us. Long ago, scientists used very simple instruments to see the positions of the planets, but that was all they could do. And then one day, in 1609, all that changed.

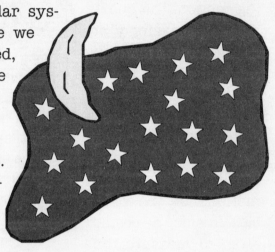

An optician's apprentice was working with various lenses while making a pair of eyeglasses. He discovered that if he placed certain lenses in certain positions and then looked through them, objects appeared closer than they actually were. This discovery was the first step toward the invention of the telescope, which used a tube-shaped body to produce an image of a faraway object. The lenses of the telescope eyepiece then magnified the image in the tube, making it appear larger and closer than it actually was.

Galileo's Discovery

Not long after 1609, an Italian mathematician and inventor named Galileo Galilei began to use the telescope to study the skies. The very first telescope was able to make objects appear thirty times their normal size. With this device, Galileo made many exciting discoveries. He saw four moons surrounding the planet Jupiter. He found spots on the surface of the sun. He proved that the Milky Way is made up of stars. And he showed the world that the sun is located at the center of our solar system. This was a startling discovery because, until then, it had always been believed that Earth itself was at the center of the solar system!

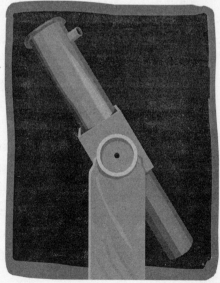

The telescope was an amazing invention

that allowed astronomers to study outer space in a whole new way. Though the first telescopes were somewhat weak, over time they became much stronger and more advanced. Today, scientists use highly advanced equipment on Earth and in outer space itself. We send telescopes into space to orbit our planet and transmit discoveries back to us through a computer. And space robots are actually sent to other planets so that we can learn more about those planets!

A CLOSER LOOK

Not long after the invention of the telescope, the instrument was adapted to create another important scientific tool. Galileo soon discovered that the telescope was not only useful for magnifying *large* objects that were far away but also tiny objects that were right here on Earth. He tinkered with his telescope and came up with a device that, as he described, could make "flies look as big as a lamb." This device was the microscope!

The first microscopes used poor-quality lenses. They could magnify an object roughly two hundred times. As time passed, scientists learned more and more about optics and how lenses work. Microscopes became increasingly powerful. By the early

1900s, microscopes could enlarge an object two thousand times.

With the help of these magnifying machines, scientists made incredible discoveries. They were able to examine all kinds of things in spectacular detail, from plants to insects to the cells that make up all living things.

Scientists found germs in contaminated drinking water. They discovered bacteria in sour milk. One of the most important discoveries made with the help of the microscope was that germs can carry disease from one person to another. Scientists began to use microscopes to study germs and bacteria. This led to the creation of vaccines: When tiny amounts of bacteria are introduced into the human body, the body builds resistance to them. The invention of vaccines has saved countless lives.

CHANGING OUR LIVES

The clock, telescope, and microscope are three incredible devices that have impacted and improved our lives. From saving lost sailors to maintaining modern medical equipment, clocks do much more than tell us the time. Telescopes allow us to make new and important discoveries about our universe every day. And without microscopes, scientists would not be able to closely examine germs, cells, and bacteria, helping us stay healthy.

Over the centuries, each of these devices has become more and more accurate, allowing us to keep track of and understand the tiniest details of both our world and our solar system.

TEST YOUR

Inventiveness!

In India in A.D. 700, Buddhist monks routinely ingested snake venom. They believed that if they were bitten, their bodies would be immune to the poison. Scientists consider this to be the first recorded attempt at immunization. True or false?

Answer: True. But nobody knows for certain whether it worked.

JUST FOR FUN:
Gadgets and Gizmos

Many inventions serve serious needs. They improve the way we live and allow scientists to do important research. Other inventions are more whimsical — they make life more interesting and more fun. These types of inventions are known as gadgets. But some gadgets can be pretty useful as well!

YOU'VE GOTTA TRY THIS

Gadgets are often little items you can hold in the palm of your hand. When you see one, you want to pick it up and try it out. It might beep or whistle, whir or buzz. It might solve a small problem or help you to do a specific task.

The very first gadgets existed as early as 2600 B.C. But the word *gadget* is a lot younger. Legend has it that the word was born in the late 1800s, when France gave the United States a famous gift: the Statue of Liberty. The grand bronze statue was conceived by the French sculptor Frederic Auguste

Bartholdi. He began work on the statue at a Parisian firm called Gaget Gautier & Cie.

The Statue of Liberty was certainly not a gadget. But the owner of the firm, Monsieur Gaget, decided to sell small replicas of Lady Liberty to excited New Yorkers, in whose city the statue found a home. Shoppers called these souvenirs "gadgets," after the man who'd created them!

Ancient Amusement

Though many think of the gadget as a modern item, ancient civilizations created small, whimsical items for amusement as well. And some of these amusing thingamajigs led the way to more serious inventions.

One such item was the Chinese magic spoon. When you threw this spoon onto the ground, it did not bounce and come to rest in a random way like an ordinary spoon. It acted as if it were possessed! No matter how or where

TEST YOUR

Inventiveness!

The Statue of Liberty is so large that it had to be packed in fifty crates to be shipped to the United States. True or false?

Answer: False. It filled two hundred crates!

you threw it, the magic spoon always landed with the bowl pointing south and the handle pointing north. This was because the magic spoons were made from magnetite, a naturally magnetic material.

The magic spoon was used as a toy and an amusement for hundreds of years. And then one day someone realized that

Imagine That!

In 1858, a man named Walter Hunt created a gadget in less than three hours. He was broke, so he sold the patent for three hundred dollars to pay off his debts. Since then, the safety pin — Walter Hunt's ingenious gadget — has made millions!

because it always pointed in the same direction, it could be used to help navigate. In the thirteenth century, the Chinese shared their magic spoon with the world — as the compass!

A GREAT GADGET SHOP

Hammacher Schlemmer is well known for its gadgets. With its flagship store located in New York City, this shop has been in existence for more than 150 years. It was originally a hardware store, and German immigrant William Schlemmer began working there was he was just twelve years old.

By the time he was thirty-one, Schlemmer was part owner along with another German immigrant named Alfred Hammacher.

At the start of the 1900s, Hammacher Schlemmer's interest turned to more unique items. The owners decided to veer away from ordinary hardware and offer more unusual fare. They advertised the first tool set for a brand-new invention — the "Horseless Carriage" (or the car). When Hammacher Schlemmer sold this item, there were fewer than six hundred automobiles in all of New York City!

Hammacher Schlemmer was the first to introduce each of a long list of inventions that have since become household essentials. The pop-up toaster, the electric shaver, the steam iron, the first cordless electric tooth-

> *Imagine That!*
>
> **In 1881 Hammacher Schlemmer began reaching a broader audience by introducing its first mail-order catalog.**

brush, the first bathroom scale, the first electric pencil sharpener, and the first automatic coffeemaker were all introduced by the famed gadget retailer.

Since its start, Hammacher Schlemmer has offered a whole host of gadgets that can be wacky and weird — but also very useful! Among these items is a computerized lawn mower that can be programmed to mow and trim a lawn all by itself. Then there is a wearable, wireless computer — complete with a fifteen-inch screen, a portable camera, and voice-recognition capabilities.

PATENT PENDING

Most gadgets that make it past the "I have a great idea" stage have patents filed in the United States Patent Office. Nearly seven million patents have been filed in the Washington, D.C., office since the system was established in 1790 under President George Washington.

Mike Colitz is a patent attorney whose job it is to search out

Imagine That!

Hammacher Schlemmer once sold a tricycle built for seven! The buyer? A pizza chain owner from San Antonio, Texas.

older patents to determine if an inventor's idea really *is* original.

Colitz has come across more than his share of what he calls "wacky patents." In fact, he's written a book called exactly that.

Some of Mike's wacky patents really *are* wacky. But, as he explains, others that seem wacky are actually quite useful.

Take chicken glasses, for instance. These are small glasses that strap onto a chicken's head! The idea may seem strange to us, but the glasses were patented in 1903 for a valid reason. Chickens do not see well and are not particularly intelligent. At feeding time they peck frantically, trying to find food on the 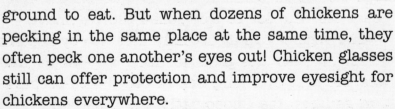 ground to eat. But when dozens of chickens are pecking in the same place at the same time, they often peck one another's eyes out! Chicken glasses still can offer protection and improve eyesight for chickens everywhere.

AS SEEN ON TV!

There is one gadgeteer who is not only famous for inventing but also for advertising his inventions. His name is Ron Popeil. If you want to be a gadget inventor, follow in his footsteps!

Popeil has invented dozens of household gadgets — items that come in handy in the kitchen or the garage. You may have even seen many of his inventions on TV.

"Ladies and gentlemen, I'm going to show you the greatest kitchen appliance ever made," Popeil said in his first television commercial. He was only twenty years old. The device was called the Vegematic.

The Vegematic was actually invented by Popeil's father. It was designed to chop vegetables and was the first in a long line of other food-preparation gadgets: the Chopomatic, the Dialamatic, and the Mincematic.

Popeil started selling his father's inventions

and later created and sold his own. It turned out he had a knack for selling useful tools and gadgets.

A popular Popeil invention was Mr. Microphone. Any kid growing up in the 1970s knew what this device was, and maybe even had one! Mr. Microphone was basically a microphone that you could plug into a radio. When you did, you were "on the air!" You could sing along and broadcast whatever you wanted through the speaker.

In 1989, the Federal Communications Commission loosened the restrictions on the length of TV commercials. Ron Popeil was

Imagine That!

One of Popeil's strangest inventions was the inside-the-egg scrambler. A tiny, motorized pin, it scrambled eggs inside the shell!

thrilled. He was marketing his Food Dehydrator at the time, and his commercials soon turned into "infomercials." Infomercials are extra-long television commercials that usually include a demonstration of how a product works. Infomercials are the perfect way to advertise gadgets!

DREAM THE DREAM

Gadgets are great. Some make our daily lives a little easier. Others tickle our funny bones. And though some gadgets are made by billion-dollar companies, many are fabricated by regular folks. A dream and determination are really all you need to create gadgets.

We've already mentioned that Hammacher Schlemmer is a great place to look if you're interested in buying a gadget. But the store also helps out gadgeteer wanna-bes. Every year the retailer hosts a Search for Invention contest. To be eligible, you first must have a patent for your gadget. Inventors can submit their gadget ideas in one of four categories: Recreation; Personal Care; Personal Electronics; and Home & Garden. The possibilities are endless! The winner of the contest receives a cash prize and the chance to sell the item in the company's catalog.

Winning the Hammacher Schlemmer contest might seem like a long shot. But you never know unless you take a chance! A school bus driver submitted his invention — an airtight container that holds collectible items (such as a signed baseball) — to the contest. Though his friends thought he was crazy to follow through with his idea, he ended up being a finalist — no small feat! Which goes to show that — regardless of what others may say — if you're a hopeful inventor, you should stay true to your vision. A concept that may seem strange to some could one day blossom into an incredible invention!

GET INVENTING

From the power of steam to the magic of movies, from the accuracy of clocks to the miracle of microscopes, history's greatest inventions all began with a seed of an idea that grew into something greater. The people behind these inventions dared to think beyond the ordinary. So if you have a passion for inventing, let these stories of inventors and their inventions be an inspiration to you!

Just think — when your parents were growing up, they most likely didn't have e-mail or easy access to the Internet. But now you — and your parents — probably can't imagine life *without* the World Wide Web! In just a small space of time, one supercool invention can make a huge difference. So what will be the groundbreaking inventions of the next generation? What sorts of tools, gadgets, instruments, or energies will revolutionize future lives in ways we never thought possible? The answer may lie in you! So what are you waiting for? It's time to get inventing!

INVENTIONS THAT ROCKED THE WORLD: THE ULTIMATE CHALLENGE

Now that you've read all about history's coolest inventions, let's see how much you remember about the various inventors and their creations!

1) A voltaic pile, one of the earliest batteries, is made up of

a. carbon filaments in a tube

b. ceramic plates and spices

c. metal plates and acid

d. waves inside a wire

2) The very first steam engines were used for

a. powering boats on the great rivers

b. passenger automobiles

c. steam trains hauling heavy loads

d. pumping water out of mines

3) Herman Hollerith invented a computer to help with

a. the U.S. Census

b. the draft

c. accounting

d. homework

**4) The first gadget Ron Popeil ever adver-
tised was**

   a. the Chopomatic

   b. Mr. Microphone

   c. the Vegematic

   d. chicken eyeglasses

**5) Henry Ford was inspired to use
assembly line production
by the**

   a. automaker Karl Benz

   b. meatpacking industry

   c. engineer James Watt

   d. railroad

**6) The mysterious ancient structure made of
stones in southern England is called**

   a. Steep Stones

   b. Stonehenge

   c. Circle of Stones

   d. Stone Soup

7) Telegraph signals had to be sent through

   a. wires

   b. smoke

   c. water

   d. pigeons

8) Many believe that the word *gadget* was coined when a Frenchman named Gaget produced and sold small replicas of
- a. the Statue of Liberty
- b. the Empire State Building
- c. the Sears Tower
- d. the Golden Gate Bridge

9) The first transistors were as big as
- a. the size of a watermelon
- b. the size of a living room
- c. the size of a finger
- d. the size of a penny

10) The person who first used telescopes to study the skies was
- a. Thomas Edison
- b. Alexander Graham Bell
- c. Benjamin Franklin
- d. Galileo Galilei

INVENTOR'S GLOSSARY

ASSEMBLY LINE [uh-SEHM-blee line]: An arranged line of machines and workers that allows work to move along until an object is assembled or completed.

ATOM [A-tuhm]: The smallest part of an element that can exist.

CARBON [KAHR-buhn]: A nonmetallic element.

CIRCUIT [SER-kit]: A path around which an electronic current can flow.

CONDUCTOR [kuhn-DUK-ter]: A substance through which electricity or heat flows with ease.

ELECTRODE [ih-LEHK-troad]: A piece of metal or carbon that collects or releases electrons in an electric circuit.

ELECTROMAGNET [ih-lehk-troh-MAG-nuht]: A core of magnetic material surrounded by a coil of wire through which an electric current is passed.

ELECTRON [ih-LEHK-trahn]: A particle in an atom with a negative electrical charge outside the nucleus.

ELEMENT [EH-luh-muhnt]: A substance that cannot be broken down into simpler substances.

FILAMENT [FIH-luh-muhnt]: A thin conductor that lights up when an electric current passes through it.

FLYWHEEL [FLY-weel]: A heavy wheel that controls the speed of the machinery of which it is part.

FREIGHT [FRAYT]: Goods or cargo transported by a vehicle or vessel.

IMMUNIZE [IH-myuh-nize]: To introduce a tiny amount of a toxin or an enzyme so that the body will produce antibodies in order to protect itself from disease.

PHOSPHORUS [FAHS-fer-uhs]: A substance that glows or lights up in the dark.

PISTON RODS [PIH-stuhn rahds]: Solid cylinders that sit inside larger cylinders and move back and forth under pressure.

PROTOTYPE [PROH-tuh-tipe]: An original model on which others are based.

QUARTZ CRYSTAL [KWORTZ KRIHS-tuhl]: A crystal that vibrates at a consistent speed; used to regulate watches and other devices.

SPECTRUM [SPEHK-truhm]: A sequence of color

formed when a beam of white light is passed through a prism.

SYNCHRONIZE [SIHN-kruh-nize]: To make two things happen at exactly the same time (such as motion picture sound and the corresponding action).

TURBINE [TUHR-buhn]: An engine put into motion by a fluid.

VACCINE [vak-SEEN]: A preparation of microorganisms that is injected into the body to help produce immunity to a given disease.